This book belongs to...

_____

Bella's Thumb Chum Trudy

By M. Fancher

Bella and Trudy are best friends, pals, chums they say! Bella and Trudy go everywhere together. They take rides in the car,

play at the park,

and even nap together.

When Bella sucks Trudy, Trudy
can't join in any of the fun.
Bella's family asks,
if you don't let Trudy out to play...

Bella, how will you
stick out your tongue?

Bella, how will we
hear your silly laugh?

One day, Bella thought it was time to let Trudy join the fun.

Trudy was so excited because now she could have fun *with* Bella!

Together, Bella and Trudy were able to show their beautiful smile!

And clap their hands!

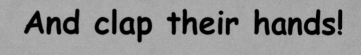

And munch on
blueberries.

And slurp soup
from the bowl!

And complete a handstand.

And brush all of her hair!

After all of the fun activities, Bella and Trudy were tired.

Yawn

Bella drank her milk before bed.

And gave her mom
a big hug before
lying down.

And while Bella was sleeping,
she dreamt about all the
fun adventures she would have with
Trudy.

What's your thumbs name?

What adventures can you and your thumb chum have?

Made in the USA
Monee, IL
28 July 2024

62798558R00017